Journey With The Ferry Man
and Other Poems

poems by

Whitney Vale

Finishing Line Press
Georgetown, Kentucky

Journey With The Ferry Man
and Other Poems

Copyright © 2016 by Whitney Vale
ISBN 978-1-944899-46-2 First Edition
All rights reserved under International and Pan-American Copyright Conventions. No part of this book may be reproduced in any manner whatsoever without written permission from the publisher, except in the case of brief quotations embodied in critical articles and reviews.

ACKNOWLEDGMENTS

The poem "The Cardiologist" was first published in the webzine, *Autumn Sky*.

Publisher: Leah Maines

Editor: Christen Kincaid

Cover Art: Whitney Vale, Sophia Lyn Sims

Author Photo: Sophia Lyn Sims

Cover Design: Elizabeth Maines

Printed in the USA on acid-free paper.
Order online: www.finishinglinepress.com
          also available on amazon.com

Author inquiries and mail orders:
Finishing Line Press
P. O. Box 1626
Georgetown, Kentucky 40324
U. S. A.

Table of Contents

Among Bright Strangers 1

Sonnet Of Light Number 3 2

In This Room, A Photograph In Black And White 3

Alice In The Looking Glass 4

Old Lovers 5

Once Upon A Time I Met A Poet And We Had 6

The Cardiologist 7

After The Film, 1986 8

Sestina: A Woman's Life 10

For The Women Of Afghanistan 12

Dogwood 13

Not Today 14

Standing In Line To Look At An Altar For Day
   Of The Dead 15

Bone 16

Journey with the Ferry Man 17

*To my husband, McCoy.
My loving companion on all my journeys.*

Among Bright Strangers

I weaved through crowds of bright
strangers, settled my child self beneath
a rack of clothes to wait, to watch for that she
among giants. The clothes a fabric forest.
I remember red, heat, muffled noise
I remember
Lost.
Panic pulsed
I stared at legs and shoe-clad feet.

Found.
A great parting of heaviness
garments shoved aside,
arms grabbed me up, rag-doll limp.
Beads of sweat on her face,
dark eyes wet, hair moist,
the smell of a long day,
cigarettes and fear clung to wool.
"Don't evers" fell
from her red mouth.

I have trouble with directions
I stand bewildered, synapses
skipping through spatial dyslexia,
my brain a confused compass.
I lift my hands, say,
"right hand", "left hand"
to orient myself.

Sometimes my vertigo pushes me right out
of my body as if some inner substance, spirit or soul,
decided to get a move on and leave me among bright strangers.

Sonnet Of Light Number 3
Viewing Black And White Photography

I started seeing geometric patterns of light 30 years ago.
I thought angels were trying to reach me
with a silent language I should be able to apprehend,
their bright symbols blinding me with blue pulsation.

Black and white pictures with their exhalations of light
remind me of Satie with his shaped pauses that are silver
geometries in my ear Da-Da-Da-Da.

Here is a study of clouds over an ocean,
puffs of grey, suspended over a streak of horizontal light,
which lie across black water,
one cloud looks like Bach.

My lights are triangles and orbs fringed in cerulean.
A doctor told me these episodes are ocular migraines
I thought he said oracular and thanked him.

In This Room, A Photograph in Black And White

She sits in profile
wearing grey
to follow her oblique gaze
is to search a haze
over a river
for
some thing actual

like a watch
               dangled
from a bare branch
that the observer could
               snatch
hold and open
pull out the parts for the how of it

he arranges her long hair over
her starved shoulder
don't move

the camera urges eternity

from the tight skin
the half smile
she looks past him

to the future
a fist of morrows
certain sorrows
hollow words

Alice in the Looking Glass

She studies her face,
naming names,
love an Etch- a-Sketch
across decades.
Alice slowly shakes her head,
perhaps the lines will drop off.

The shadow under the right eye
belongs to the married man,
under the left is the bruise of incest,
the raised vertical lines
between her sparring brows
trace a child lost behind mirrors.

She tumbles down a memory
as she glosses her lips
first kissed by that boy across the street—
she loved his brother.
The brick wall warm behind her back
his mouth sudden and feathery
then he was gone
teenage boy gone
to sports and blondes.

Alice plucks a hair, and sees
a tiny drop of blood, pure red
as in the first time of shared sheets—
he was a carpenter with rough hands,
a foreign name, a winged tattoo.

Alice looks at her aging face, beauty
broken like a fragmented butterfly.
She pushes blush into a mirage.

When she stares into her eyes
neither sex stares back, but a bird
lured to earth, laying tracks.

Old Lovers

Patrick, the Viking,
Merlot drunk, loved poetry

Richard, who sat
On hot June nights in front of his open fridge
To scorn the teaching of thrifty parents

Logan, tall in light
Short in fidelity

I loved them
Their masculine imperative to divide
Hesitation and assume surrender

I loved the Viking's soft sigh
Richard's green eyed lies
Logan's metaphysical dance

They all brought me here
To the woman I am
Who cries at sunset and laughs at rain
Who dances on gravel
And praises the hunting owl

Once Upon a Time I Met a Poet And We Had

sex in the afternoon… I lit a candle.

As you expressed yourself I recalled… Narcissus
I nodded at words that leapt like dying salmon:

>You saw one of my poems tacked to a wall in the kitchen—
>pointed to a line you liked
>nodded to yourself nodded to me… raised an eyebrow—

the next day I went to a bookstore and saw your book
read it cover to cover. It was short.

You never came back…
and I wondered what I wanted—
a phone call
or my own place on a shelf that didn't smell of old dreams.

>I wondered if you would remember the moment of that
>good line and

use it like you used me—

but it's ok

because here you are again, Narcissus
and at any moment I can delete you.

The Cardiologist

I was felt up by the heart man.
His dangling stethoscope,
brought to attention by his trembling hand.
Its round, flat, cold tip
found the soft palpitation
beneath my blue denim dress.
He pressed.
He pressed here.
He pressed there.
(And I gazed inward into my left chamber
and placed a laugh there which confused his science a little.)

And all because I have a smart mouth.
A mouth that is sometimes red, pink, or shiny.
A mouth that purses, and drops its coin of Puckish humor,
like when I said when I stopped smoking I stopped writing poetry,
so really, *got a light?*

He said, so what, take up something else,
like sewing, or men.
I said, *oh really?* I did that, I'm married now.
That's when he whipped it out, still limp, and snapped
me up to the paper couch, and grabbed at past heart beats,
listening for the memory of heat.

And so I laughed inside at his youth,
'cause I know a thing or two about hearts myself.

I turned down the procedure that would kill off
my extra nerve, figuring
I would need it to spark my mouth.
Later, in the car, I lit an American Spirit,
and followed the smoke signals down the Red Road,
and the drums began.

After The Film, 1986

I tilt down La Brea frightened,
the way women get, you know,
all manner of men ogre-ing in alleys
even on a sunny LA day, Blue Velvet
hurt my head, fractured balance, I trip

down La Brea from the Boulevard
side-step shards of glass,
I stop
when I see a photograph face up
in an ill-kempt yard, glowing in Pepsodent perfection.
I walk faster trying to shake off

Dennis Hopper, a bruised Rossellini,
those smiles gleaming from the dirt.
Find myself in front of a small nursery
on the corner of La Brea and Santa Monica,
sweating in the heat. Air conditioning,
the smell of earth compels me enter, I cross

over a little white bridge,
still under a celluloid cloud,
there is fake turf before the entrance,
small garden gnomes grin and squat
on fake hillocks. A plaster swan has a cracked wing.
I'm in Hollywood. It doesn't mean anything
unless you believe in salvation,

maybe Jesus sleeps in miniature roses
and Birds of Paradise, and maybe camellias
restore the soul, and maybe there is something
about earth and seed that softens despair,
the way a good tilling works the greening deep.

Relief shivers in little ferny fronds down my spine,
a walk through each aisle stacked with flower trays
feels like a petal handkerchief,
and my balance returns as I cross the bridge
back to the hot street of concrete and broken glass,
balance returns as I continue home,
a potted geranium held to my heart.

Sestina: A Woman's Life

I look around my room and see my life
on tables laden with notebooks and cups of pens,
bulletin boards collaged by calendar and bright verse,
books Pisa towered next to a velvet cushion,
book shelves sag with memento and literary weight,
while in an undusted corner leans a silver star.

The closet holds theatrical histories from when I was a star,
there are plays, masks, personas from a life
of sprung rhythms and exclamation marks, *wait!*
cried ingénue me, and I sang in the Pirates of Penz-
ance. I hope this collected stuff will cushion
the vagaries of years or fuel the files of verse

that whisper *sotto voce* and converse
with the chipped plaster fairy, a star
of the third shelf who sits next to the pin cushion
where I stick snapshots of my present life.
My black cat leaps like poetry—scatters my pens,
as I throw up my hands to catch his old weight

he twists like a moebius strip, will he wait
midair, boundless and free, will he be adverse
to my aid, hiss disdain, not give a copper pence?
He eludes me, indeed, knocks over my silver star
runs pursued by ghosts of a fiction's life.
Would I do that too? Oh, if I could shun

these clouds of witness, lay down upon the cushion…
no, I walk the path around the room, wait
for angels to land in trees and give me a new life
so I may snip pics and words, be well versed
in the ways of aging well, and be rinsed clean as a star
roaming free of orbital pens.

Here I am wondering, on needles and pins—
if I can begin again, surrounded by the cushion
of mystery and art , can I make a fresh start? Star
in a new cosmic dance? So I've put on weight
so what, there's no gravity in dreams, quite the reverse
I'll float like a skylark through this cerulean life.

"A Woman's Life". The skylark pens
her verse while eating *bons mots* on a cushion
the song's weight is light as a star.

For The Women of Afghanistan
After the landay, a traditional oral poem

Woman, your red voice will bite the stricken wind
Blue shrouds swirling cannot strangle your harsh art.

Dogwood

Mother carried a song in her square hands
One evening she beckoned, she called, she crooned
Our way out doors into the southern stillness
Two saplings leaned against a chain link fence

Into the backyard of empty spaces we went
Under a pitch of stars we dug
We pulled out earth around us, a circle
I think we dug to China

I remember only silence
Or perhaps we spoke
Perhaps she hummed
I remember wet earth
The grunt of effort
I remember an air of tenderness
In the deepening dusk

Burlap wombs were set in the ground
The trees took
Roots inched through rough sack
To suckle the place of nourishment

My adult hands tingle as I recall
The first fall of blossom in spring
Pink fleshy petals drop from my palm
Over a name on unpolished granite

Carolyn had secrets
Songs hummed never sung aloud
Uncanny, bigger than her life
Some women should never be wife
Mother of dwindled choices, Carolyn
Oh, she danced in her dreams with sailors
Trees uprooted to partner her,
Oceans parted; oh, she was a wild one,
Wild beneath the earth, taking the moon with her

Not Today

The day of your funeral the wild came forward
Two mallards lifted in the distance and slowly ascended
Breaking through clouds, emerald heads flashing light

Your blind dog limped a path from bed to chair noting
Absence, hearing the muffled cry of a yonder place
Finally lying down with paws crossed, lost in silence

An indigo butterfly circled the air on the patio
Sipping cigarette smoke and sugar, chased by a child
Who knows only life and laughter

Jays and robins quarreled over who loved you best
There was a blue feather in my door handle
Rabbits overcame fear to remain in view

And there on the green, ants carried messages through blades
Of remorse, lions travelled from Africa, tigers and orangutans
Removed maps from walls and circled the globe to hear the weeping

Many mornings after the earth was dug and filled, and some mornings
Still, I awake and think today is the day of your return, the hawks
Cry it is not so, the loudness of life in the air sings not today, not today.

Standing in Line to Look at an Altar for Day of the Dead

Bone drew this forth
Bone of sea
Bone of fire
Bone of earth

Black cloth and white bone
Chalk made from layers of passing
(Dover erodes
The sea is triumphant and the sea mourns)

White lines blurred by association
Chalk fingers sketch portraits of loss
Dust to dust

Black cloth black water
Ebbs eddies puddles to the floor

What scenes propel the invisible
Photographs fade
Memories ground to powder

I can't read the ghost bone writing
I can graze the lines of witness
I can grace the line of waiting
There is always a boat
(I can hear the sea at Dover)
I can see the body's velvet cloth erode over time

One night in D.C.
Driving by the Potomac
All I could feel was terror as I imagined
The bottomless river lapping black lapping black
Against the white bone of my fear

Bone

Woolf's Black Dog
digs a hole in my backyard,
plants a gnawed white bone.

It worries my dreams
my day   my breath.

Dog
you are black crepe,
foul breath that chokes my voice.

I go out there
on hands and knees, scrape
away gravel, sniff that bone out
grab it with my teeth and yank.

I pant, whine, growl.
It is in my lap,
debris clings
to its pitted surface.
Bone
stained with my life.

Journey with the Ferry Man

Prelude

Isolate
This lady of white hands
Sits inert before the glass,
Agility slowed
One hand caresses blank paper.
What passes through reflection is fluttered fear, revealed at last
Her fear of death

Black pen in the right
She grasps for mirrors, myths and makes belief the peak against the vale

What sustains is tension, a line wrought where thoughts converge, volute
And constellate around a portion of night in the glass

And she so thirsty in her reverie
Flashing curiosities
Integrated fragments, narratives that thrum
That flame the will and rebel
To sound out contradiction
Quests not shunned

It proves a long night of years to this point
Urge the asking
Tremble on the tongue

Psyche had 4 tasks
How many, how many do I?

1.

Which waking is real?

2.

Throw me some black bread that I may feed
Ebony ants for my struggle, here now, as I separate
Tenses and sources, the boy is gone, the girl is going

Amour, Ardor, Amative

3.

4 tasks:
Sort seeds, gather Golden Fleece, fill a flask from the river Styx,

walk to Hell
And bring back a box of beauty

4.

O!
I remember that Old Gal, Mother Love all right
Her frets and jealousies, her deep sea dreams and drowning

5.

She/ me—O! I then
Cull from the scattered bits
Perilous
Love! Beauty! Truth!

I sit among heaps of conceits
The golden fleece deep piling.

Patience is no virtue to desire—
I ache within this flesh for that remembered grove

For a taste of beauty I will soak bread in honey
And drop a loaf
To the water

A loaf to the hands
A loaf to the dogs that howl—

Love is not always kind nor beauty a pretty sight
I howl back.

Crawl and grub to the grove
Assisted by ants who see atoms
Pursued by rivalry and devilry
Within the grove I will build
A haloed habitat

6.
In transit, mute, searching for trans
Port
By air, or bus

A way back home

Trans substance… a way across… or through
The confinement of mundane masks
Inferior tasks

7.

Tree of thorns, mind
A burst of fragile blossoms
Float into the breeze
All I have is this love, god
This force that compels migration

This love which takes me through the glass
My lamp
My heart

My desire that melts as wax upon my nakedness

8.

Another circling around and around (and around it)
One task for me, beneath the arc
^
Tend to words
Compose my line's tenacity though slender needles pin me down

Set out shallow bowls of sweet water
For traveling, sip
From depressions on the ground, rip
Elusive allusions to their roots

Dream inner verdancy, drums
Through text
Electric, clamant

Carry on and carry back
Through links of kore/woman/poet
Raise papery wings

9.

There is a graveyard
Where celebrated actors of classic film lay interred
By lagoons and reflecting pools
Marble women weep
                        prostrated for eternity
I walked there long ago
                        seeing through fretwork shadows

Canova's sculpture: Psyche Revived By Cupid's Kiss
I walked around it and around (and around it)
                             beneath a flowering almond I touched
The hard white thigh
Of Eros
And traced the stretched muscles of Psyche's   reaching arms

Nearby, a movie studio winds film and dreams in metal caskets

You can see the white signage of the hills in the polluted distance

10.

I have walked by Tanque Verde wash, dry river
Counted the marbleized patterns left by old rains
Smelled the rising scent of piss left
By a thousand ghost dogs
I have heard the echoing yip of the coyote from the vaulted aqueduct
I have sighed into myself as the many headed dog of youth
Rushed across the stricken field

11.

I unfold
Into books, circle hard words, underline passages,
Collect prettiness
For index cards
Decipher in a wondering way:

"The pelvis is a pre-lapse double wing
Resembles a calcified –"

"Psyche means soul and butterfly in Greek"

"Poet—
 means maker"

"Rouse—
to ruffle the feathers of a hawk"

That bitch Aphrodite

Chant songs of childsense
Sticks and stones may break my bones
And words will ever wound me

I stare at this poem, watching
Like I am training a wild hawk

12.

Instead of coins, I will give the Ferry Man
Two poems
One for each hand
And we will glide by the singing weeds
And I will hold a signing reed

13.

I was a little girl on a hill
Frozen in fear on a hill on Grandpa's farm
We were going to the waterfall
Terror rooted me, it was autumn

Fill the vessel with water, Psyche
There was no eagle to help me
I could only fill my hands with my own tears
There on the hill
My hands full of my escape from the fear of falling

Grandpa warned of snakes
There be dragons… Watch out for rattlers
Grandpa seed one as thick as his arm

I found a geode on the side of the hill
Grandpa offered to break it in two
I know it is full of condensed water and light

I have it now, I am holding it now

14.

My thoughts are fritillaries searching for passion flowers

15.

Don't open the box of beauty it is full of sleep

Artist Statement

The first poem I recall hearing was by Ogden Nash, the second was by Edgar Allen Poe. Both were read aloud while I was in the first grade. What I remember was the musicality of language, and that language was woven through narrative. Every poem for me begins as a lyric impulse, and as a desire to share a story. That story may have narrator following a sparrow, or exploring the body of an aging woman. What holds these two tales together is an appreciation of sound. As a non musician, I use words to make up for that lack of training. I think that sound can carry the emotive self into a field of understanding that circumvents the intellect.

Additional Acknowledgments

I extend my deep appreciation for the staff of the Poetry Center at the University of Arizona, in particular, Tyler Meier and Cybele Knowles. I am eternally grateful to former staff member, Julie Lauterbach-Colby.

I extend my warm regards and rosy thank-yous to the Poetry Center Writer's Workshop, led by Ken Lamberton. This group of varied voices has been inspiring. They are: Walker Thomas, Gillian Haines, Billy Sedlmayr, Ralph Hager, Tyler Atkinson, Barbara Peabody, Klara Lynn Dannar, Jerry Whitney, Sarah Spieth, and Laurie Calland.

I am grateful to all my teachers over the years, and in particular I am indebted to Rebecca Seiferle for her workshop, The Poem Sequence, and her attention to Journey with the Ferry Man.

My heartfelt thanks to Finishing Line Press for selecting this manuscript for publication.

And most of all, I acknowledge with love and pride, my husband, McCoy.

Whitney Vale is a docent at the University of Arizona's Poetry Center in Tucson. Via the docent program she is also a member of the Speaker's Bureau, a committee dedicated to bringing poetry out into the Tucson community through poetry readings and facilitated conversation. Whitney was a finalist for the 2014 Joy Harjo Poetry Award. She has been published on AutumnSkyPoetry.com and in the anthology, *Inside: out*.

Whitney was awarded a Master of Fine Arts in Acting from Catholic University, Washington D.C. She has acted in regional theatres on both coasts, and was in the inaugural professional apprentice program at Actors Theatre in Louisville, KY. Her favorite role there was in *Marat/Sade*, where she enjoyed scaring the patrons and wearing their winter coats during intermission. During a varied work career, Whitney has sold candy (and eaten a fair amount), sofas and vitamins. She performed stand-up and caught a few laughs. She has been a waitress and a short order cook—for a short amount of time. She also worked in film exhibition and distribution in Los Angeles. She is currently in Level 1 Teacher Training for Kundalini Yoga, and is a licensed life coach. Whitney is working on a second manuscript, *A Memoir of Dance*. Her life is illuminated by the presence of her husband, William McCoy.

www.ingramcontent.com/pod-product-compliance
Lightning Source LLC
Chambersburg PA
CBHW060227050426
42446CB00013B/3200